Living With The Mind of A Reprobate

By
Karen M. Radcliff

To order additional copies of this book, contact:
Xlibris
844-714-8691
www.Xlibris.com
Orders@Xlibris.com

Scripture quotations marked KJV are from the Holy
Bible, King James Version (Authorized Version).
First published in 1611. Quoted from the KJV
Classic Reference Bible, Copyright © 1983 by The
Zondervan Corporation.

ISBN: Softcover   978-1-6698-5358-9
       EBook   978-1-6698-5359-6

Print information available on the last page

Rev. date: 10/28/2022

Table of Contents

Part I –

INTRODUCTION

Jeremiah 29:11 states, "For I know the plans I have for you declares the Lord, plans to prosper you and not harm you, plans to give you hope and a future."

Let's begin with the definition of a **reprobate**:

The expression "reprobate mind" is observed in Romans 1:28 (KJV) relating to those who God has denied as godless and wicked. They "suppress the truth by their wickedness," and it is against these people that the wrath of God occurs (Romans 1:18). The Greek word translated "reprobate" in the New Testament is *adokimos*, which means "unapproved, refused; by implication, worthless."

1

When one continuously rejects God after having accepted Him in the pardon of their sins, and after a period of time rejects His Word, this is one of the consequences he/she will encounter.

Watching a loved one who once professed the Lord Jesus Christ as their personal Savior stray away from God can be very discouraging and disheartening. One may ask, "How did this happen?" I assure you that this doesn't happen overnight. If you pay attention there are signs of this behavior long before the person gets to this place. Sometimes it can take years before the mind of the reprobate to show up!

What happens when the mind becomes distorted? The answer is, it happens when we as Christians no longer put Christ as the head of our lives. Like the Children of Israel, we begin to place other things before Him. Such as careers, food, alcohol, drugs, husband, wives, children, homes, and anything else before Him! Exodus 20:3 (KJV) states, "Thou shalt have no other gods before me." And this is basically how it begins. The enemy of soul, the flesh, is getting pampered, nourished, fed what it wants, and the mind begins to say, "I'd rather have that than God's Word!" He/she starts to move away from God, and without realizing they have become, "Backsliders!" Jeremiah 3:14 (KJV) says: "'Return, O backsliding children,' says the Lord; 'for I am married to you. I will take you, one from a city and two from a family, and I will bring you to Zion.'". The sense that is conveyed in this scripture passage is that the Lord is the husband over his people; he is the master over them and in control. For the people's part, they didn't treat God as their husband but ran after other gods who were worthless.

The God that we serve is truly a merciful God. He will give us the time that we need to get our house in order. But, God is also a gentleman, He will not infringe Himself on anyone. It is up to the person to repent and ask God for forgiveness, and allow Him into their lives.

Part II -

FOOD ADDICTION

Let's look at the idolization regarding food. The scripture says, "Listen my son and be wise, and set not your heart on the right path: Do not join those who drink too much wine or gorge themselves on meat, for drunkards and gluttons become poor, and drowsiness clothes them in rags." Proverbs 23:19-20 (NIV)

There are many variables that can be entered into when food becomes our, "god" such as:
- Idolatry - Exodus 20:2
- Treating your body poorly. 1 Corinthians 6:19

- Giving into temptation and the desires of the flesh. Proverbs 4:14-15
- Lacking self-control. Proverbs 25:28; 1 Corinthians 10:13; Galatians 5:22-23

So, "What is happening to this spirit-filled believer?" The answer is he/she is taking on the mind of a reprobate. James 1:8 (KJV) states. "A double minded man is unstable in all his ways." Instability can certainly lead to having a reprobate mind when one chooses to serve the "flesh" rather than choosing to serve God! We all have a choice, and it's a personal choice. Over a period of time he/she will no longer fight for their lives, but will consistently give in to the cravings of the flesh. Without the, " parakletos" the Holy Spirit - which means in Greek, "the one called to help alongside" we will not be able to fight addictions. This is when a war erupts. The flesh is battling with the Spirit to conquer the mind of the individual it once had! When food and gluttony is put in the place of God, the person can rest assured that there are some dangerous health issues that will erupt. "Whose end is destruction, whose God is their belly, and whose glory is in their shame, who mind earthly things." (Philippians 3:19) Food like most addictions can cause the person to engage in many damnable situations. These negative spirits will work hand in hand to satisfy the flesh. The person will lie, cheat and steal if they have to to get exactly what they want. Food cravings increase especially for the types of food the person likes. If the person likes pizza, soda, bacon, etc. those cravings will begin to overtake them. The person that is designated to grocery shopping cannot allow themselves to become an enabler. An enabler is one who provides for the person in self destructive behavior. For example, how many times has a person purchased cigarettes for a loved one, friend, etc. knowing that they have cancer. The person has to ask God for strength to help them look past the person with the reprobate mind, take a stand to do what is right.

Part III -

RECOGNITION

It is astonishing how you can live, eat and sleep with someone who attends church regularly, yet their relationship with God is diminishing day by day. If you are **living with the mind of a reprobate**, behaviors on your part will have to change. You do not have the communication skills you once had when you were in agreement with one another. Amos 3:3 (KJV) states, "Can two walk together, except they be agreed?" The answer to this question is no. We must remember that we cannot force God on anyone, nor can we force anyone to serve God! Looking to God for instructions regarding our lives is now impeccable. In order to move forward, we need assurance on how to move, when to move, and when to be still. Most importantly we must learn when and when not to speak. Knowing this, and by giving our mouths over to the Holy Spirit will allow the peace of God to abide with us at all times. Isaiah 26:3 (KJV) states, " I will keep him in perfect peace whose mind is stayed on thee, because he trusteth in thee." In order to maintain a civil relationship while **living with the mind of a reprobate** one **MUST** submit themselves to God daily. If you are not willing to submit, you are in for utter chaos in your life. Don't get it twisted, **living with the mind of a reprobate** can cause you to become crazy if you're not careful. Most of us have experienced that old saying, " misery loves company."

Part IV -

LYING

It is imperative that we pay attention to the behavior of a person who has a reprobate mind. Ninety percent of the time if the person has continued to rebel against God, negative **spirits** will begin to manifest in that person. When the person refuses to face the truth they will lie. Lying itself is an act of betrayal, and it violates the trust your friend, spouse, or family member is trying to build with you. When people uncover lies, depending on how damaging the lies are, some relationships become ruined beyond repair. The definition of lie and or lying is to practice deceit, falsehood, and treachery either by word or action. It is the exact opposite of truth. The sanctity of truth is fundamental in biblical teaching since it is based on the nature and character of God (Num 23:19 ; 1 Sam 15:29 ; Rom 3:4 ; Titus 1:2 ; Heb 6:18 .

The person will usually lie to cover up the truth, so they won't have to face reality. The only thing is. the person will have to remember the lie in order to cover it up. This behavior will prompt the person to continue to lie, therefore lying then becomes habitual. The person is in constant denial, and at some point may not remember the lies he/she told. Behavior is also a form of detecting when a person is lying. These are a few ways one can detect when a person is lying:

1. Being vague; offering few details.
2. Repeating questions before answering them.
3. Speaking in sentence fragments.
4. Failing to provide specific details when a story is challenged.
5. Grooming behaviors such as playing with hair or pressing fingers to lips.

As Christians God we have a greater gift, and that is being able to **discern** when a person is lying. Discernment simply means that one is able to distinguish, separate out by didgent search, or examine.

Discernment involves perception along with insight. "Moreover, they shall teach My people the difference between the holy and the profane, and cause them to discern between the unclean and the clean." Ezekiel 44:33 (KJV) It can become tedious to communicate with a person who lies the majority of the time. You can have a conversation, but it will be limited. When health issues are involved, the person who is the caregiver may choose consulting with the doctor(s). Developing a good rapport with those in the medical field will certainly enhance the truth about what's really going on. You may also have family members or friends that are in the medical field. This can be an asset as well. It is vital that we seek God's wisdom for handling **every** situation. **Living with the mind of a reprobate** is not easy, and after a period of time it can be dangerous. When he/she desires are not met, they can and will seek a way out of the relationship. They will go as far as seek assistance from their family along with the court in getting a person out of the home and out of their lives..

Part V -
ATTENTION SEEKING

When you are **living with the mind of a reprobate**, the person may show signs of attention seeking behavior. An attention seeker is someone who acts solely in a way that is geared towards garnering the attention of other people. The attention they receive makes them feel better about themselves, boosts their self-esteem, and it doesn't matter if that attention is good or bad. If this behavior is tolerated it can become manipulative and harmful. Here are a few characteristics relating to an attention seeker:

1. Persistently bragging.
2. Fishing for compliments.

3. Professional victim.
4. Constant complainer.
5. Never a dull moment. Consistent drama.

Years ago there was a commercial that stated, "A mind is a terrible thing to waste!" The commercial was making reference to drug use, and its effects. When Chritians reject God after knowing Him our minds begin to deteriorate just like any other disease that inflicts our bodies, This gradually happens with the person not realizing how far they've strayed away from God, and His ordinances. The truth/ God the person once knew has now become a lie/ Satan! "Lying lips are an abomination to the LORD: but they that deal truly are his delight." Proverbs 12:22 (KJV).

A person who is seeking constant attention can be labeled as having a personality disorder. This personality disorder is called, "Histrionic Personality Disorder." This disorder shows up through a deliberate display of emotions and theatrics. The person will start crying after being told the truth, seemingly signifying that he/she is sorry for their actions, etc. The person will lie about their health issues. For example - the person fell and bruised their ankle, but to get sympathy they will state that they " broke" their ankle to make the situation appear worse than it is. Their self-esteem relies on the approval of others, and therefore it does not come from a **true** feeling of self worth!

Part VI -

NON-CARING

We must make sure that our self-esteem is intact. In order to continue in the relationship with the one who is of a reprobate mind we must read and study the Word of God daily. 2 Timothy 2:15, (KJV)"Study to show thyself approved unto God, a workman that needed not to be ashamed, rightly dividing the word of truth." Fasting and prayer are an essential part of our daily routine. We must stand firm on God's word not wavering, no matter the cost. Having God's unconditional love manifested in and through us will allow us not to focus on the negative, but continuously seek the good in every situation. We cannot let the person who has the mind of a probate bring us down to their level. Ephesians

6:14, (KJV) "Stand therefore having your loins girt about with truth, and having on the breastplate of righteousness;" "Gird up your loins," simply means that one is well prepared for the challenges ahead. In a marriage the majority of havel stood before God, witnesses and vowed to love each other in sickness and in health; for better or worse, and for richer and poorer. The question one then has to ask themselves is, "Why did I marry this person?" He or she will systematically have to answer this question in order to have the capability of moving forward. Moving forward is essential for every believer because it is the goal of the enemy to keep us stagnated. They will constantly inflict guilt, anger, frustration, and anything else that will keep our minds bogged down, and the focus on ourselves. We must always keep our focus on God by redirecting our thoughts. Philippians 4:8, (KJV) "Finally, brethren, whatsoever things are true, whatsoever things are honest, whatsoever things are just, whatsoever things are pure, whatsoever things are lovely, whatsoever things are of good report; if there be any virtue, and if there be any praise, think on these things." We must redirect our minds, behaviors, attitudes, conversations, etc, on these things listed above. God is always present, listening, and ready to help us through all of our trials and tribulations.

Part VII -

VALIDITY

Definition of validity: the quality or state of being valid : such as a: the state of being acceptable according to the law The validity of the contract is being questioned.

In nature, there are four types of validity that are used in research. They are as follows:

1. Construct validity refers to what we are interested in.
2. Content validity refers to measuring the mood,
3. Face validity refers to subjective and informal assessment.
4. Criterion validity refers to the external measurement of a similar thing.

Self-validation is accepting your own internal experience, your thoughts, and your feelings. Self-validation doesn't mean that you believe your thoughts or think your feelings are justified. There are many times that you will have thoughts that surprise you or that don't reflect your values or what you know is true.

According to scripture, Jesus Christ has already validated us when we accept Him as our Lord and Savior. 2 Corinthians 5:17 (KJV) states, "If any man be in Christ he is a new creature, old things are passed away; behold all things are become new." Romans 5:1(KJV) states, "Therefore being justified by faith we have peace with God through our Lord Jesus Christ." No matter how often Satan, our accuser tries to do everything he can to destroy our integrity, supposition, precondition, and our relationship with God, we must hold fast, and hold on.

Part VIII -

SANCTIONING

Another word for sanction is authority. **Living with the mind of a reprobate** will cause one to recognize the mindset when trying to reason . The person will believe that he/she is right, have authority even when they are in the wrong, and will refuse to apologize when the truth has been established.

Sanctions, in law and legal definition, are penalties or other means of enforcement used to provide incentives for obedience with the law, or with rules and regulations. Criminal sanctions can take the form of serious punishment, such as corporal or capital punishment, incarceration, or severe fines. Spiritually this can cause death or life, heaven or hell.

A person with a reprobate mind will believe he/she won't receive any consequences for their actions, and will endorse others to take part in their quest. When this happens the person involved must make a decision. That decision is to obey God or not. Depending upon the circumstances he/she may have to flee the situation. The enemy, Satan, is very cunning in regards to his tactics. One must be able to hear the voice of God and be ready to move expeditiously. Ephesians 6:11-12 (KJV) states, "Put on the whole armor of God that ye may be able to stand against the wiles of the devil." "For we wrestle not against flesh and blood, but against principalities, rulers of darkness of this world, against spiritual wickedness in high places.

Part IX –

FINALLY

Ephesians 6:10 (KJV) states, "Finally my brethren be strong in the Lord, and in the power of His might!" It is going to take the strength of God, the power of the Holy Ghost, and it will certainly take courage to get through when you are **living with the mind of a reprobate.** Joshua 1:9 (KJV) states, Have not I commanded thee? Be strong and of a good courage; be not afraid, neither be thou dismayed: for the Lord thy God is with thee whithersoever thou goest. It is apparent that we fine tune our ears to God's voice. We must submit our whole being to Him and to His Word. The sting of lies, betrayal, mistrust, and abuse will heal over time. We must govern ourselves according to scripture, and most of

all to the will of God for our lives. Think about it, Jesus went through far worse than we could imagine. As we rise to see brand new days, we nust gird up our loins, and put on the whole armor of God! Ephesians 6:11-12 (KJV) states, "Put on the whole armor of God, that ye may be able to stand against the wiles of the devil. For we wrestle not against flesh and blood, but against principalities, against powers, against the rulers of the darkness of this world, against spiritual wickedness in high places." We are at war, and we must be ready for whatever the devil will throw at us. Too many of us chritians are being caught off guard. This is not acceptable when the bible states in 2 Corinthians 2:11 (KJV) "Lest Satan should get an advantage of us: for we are not ignorant of his devices." Don't allow the enemy to get the upper hand. Fight the good fight of faith, stand on the Word of God, keep the faith, and he, (Satan) will have to return back to hell from whence he came. In most cases there will be no return to the situation God has delivered you from. Most of all we must love and pray for our enemies, and all those who despitefully use us, and say all manner of evil against us.

Part X –

CONCLUSION

Having to start over is not easy. Just know that God is able to keep you in perfect peace as we keep our minds stayed on Him. Isaiah 26:3 (KJV) states,"Thou wilt keep him in perfect peace, whose mind is stayed on thee: because he trusteth in thee." The hurt may sting to one's core. Having to flee from a reprobate may cost you to lose everything, but remember God is a restorer! He is able to give back everything that was lost, and more. But we must first forgive, not for the one who hurt us, but for ourselves. Satan would love to keep us in bondage, through our thoughts. He will consistently bager you by memory. Philippians 4:8 (KJV) states, "Finally, brethren, whatsoever things are true, whatsoever things are honest, whatsoever things are just, whatsoever things are pure, whatsoever things are lovely, whatsoever things are of good report; if there be any virtue, and if there be any praise, think on these things." 1everytime the enemy brings negative thoughts to mind regarding the situation, we must retaliate by declaring and decreeing the Word of God just like Jesus did!

Father in the name of Jesus. I thank you that I made it out! It is only because of your grace and mercy that I found the strength to endure this situation. Your Holy Ghost power gave me the ability to move forward, and is keeping me from looking back. I thank you that in the days, weeks, months, and years to come I will not only be healed, but made completely whole again. For I will recognize more and more each day what your Word states in Isaiah 54:17, "No weapon that is formed against thee shall prosper; and every tongue that shall rise against thee in judgment thou shalt condemn. This is the heritage of the servants of the Lord, and their righteousness is of me, saith the Lord." As I continue to absorb Your Word dear Lord, and apply it everyday in my life I am, and will always be a CONQUEROR! I am free, no longer bound by, **"Living With the Mind of a Reprobate!"**

Printed in the United States
by Baker & Taylor Publisher Services